READ MUSIC: IN 1 DAY

2 Manuscripts in 1 Book, Including: How to Read Music and How to Play Piano

Preston Hoffman

More by Preston Hoffman

Discover all books from the Music Best Seller Series by Preston Hoffman at:

bit.ly/preston-hoffman

Book 1: *Music Theory*

Book 2: *How to Read Music*

Book 3: *How to Play Guitar*

Book 4: *How to Play Ukulele*

Book 5: *How to Play Piano*

Book 6: *How to Play Chords*

Book 7: *How to Play Scales*

Themed book bundles available at discounted prices:

bit.ly/preston-hoffman

Table of Contents

HOW TO READ MUSIC: IN 1 DAY 5
HOW TO PLAY PIANO: IN 1 DAY 66

BOOK 1
HOW TO READ MUSIC: IN 1 DAY

The Only 7 Exercises You Need to Learn Sheet Music Theory and Reading Musical Notation Today

Preston Hoffman

Table of Contents

Introduction 8

Chapter One: Fundamentals of Music Theory 10

Chapter Two: Fundamentals of Music Notation 36

Chapter Three: Elements of Reading Sheet Music 54

Chapter Four: Seven Step-by-Step Exercises to Help You Learn How to Read Sheet Music 59

Conclusion 64

© Copyright 2017 - All rights reserved.

It is not legal to reproduce, duplicate, or transmit any part of this document in either electronic means or in printed format. Recording of this publication is strictly prohibited.

Introduction

Music can be described as a chronological organization of sounds to create a beautiful form that is melodic, rhythmic and harmonious. Music has been a part of human culture long before recorded culture. It unifies the mind and soul and helps people express emotion. In the early days before the invention of audio recording and playback, people came up with a way of writing music as a way of communicating and preserving it. Written music is also referred to as sheet music. Written music language has been around for almost as long as the normal language we use to speak. It has undergone constant development through thousands of years. The written music language we use today has been around for over three decades.

Written music language is based on a system of notation that provides musicians with all the information they require to play a piece of music in the same way the composer intended it to be played. Music notation is a system that uses symbols to represent sounds and other aspects of music, such as timing, pitch, and duration. Music notation can also be used to represent more advanced aspects of music such as timbre, expression, and even special musical effects.

Learning how to read sheet music can be a bit of a challenging task, in particular for people who have not attended any prior music lessons. Like with learning most other skills, it is important to realize that there is no magic bullet for learning how to read music. However, with practice, anyone can learn how to read music, especially when it is broken down into small, simple steps.

This book will give you an introduction to the basics of reading music, give you a basic understanding of the fundamentals of music theory and notation and the elements of reading sheet music. It will also give you simple, step-by-step exercises that will help you learn how to read sheet music in one day.

Chapter One: Fundamentals of Music Theory

Before getting into sheet music and how it is written and read, it is important to have a very, very solid understanding of music theory. Music theory looks at various aural phenomena and how they are applied in music. It also considers the reasoning behind music – what makes music work as well as the rules followed by composers when creating music. Here are the basic aural phenomena that constitute the fundamentals of music.

Pitch

Pitch is a measure of how high or low a tone is. While pitch can be accurately measured, music theorists consider pitch to be subjective. This is because most natural sounds are comprised of a complex mix of several frequencies. In music, letter names are used to represent some specific frequencies. For instance, in most orchestras, the frequency of 440 HZ is referred to as the Concert A. However, this is not standard. There are no hard rules on how to assign letter names to different frequencies.

Most cultures allow pitch to vary in different pieces of music depending on mood, style, and genre. If you go back to France in the 1850's, the A represented 435 Hz.

However, there is a specific convention that is followed. Pitches are assigned the first seven letters of the alphabet, from A all the way to G, with A representing the lowest pitch and G representing the highest pitch. Pitches higher than G start over again at A but with a higher octave. Pitches with the same name but different octaves are referred to as a pitch class. A frequency difference between two pitches is known as an interval.

Intervals

An interval refers to the distance between two pitches. Interval names consist of a number and a prefix. The number denotes the number of pitch names between the two pitches. For instance, there are two pitch names between the whole step F to G. These two pitch names are F and G. Since this interval has two pitches names, it is known as a second. However, the interval from F to A has three pitches; F, G and A. This interval is therefore known as a third. This goes on until we get to the pitch interval with eight pitch names. Intervals with eight pitch names (for instance, F to F or A to A) are known as octaves. Intervals between two notes of the exact same pitch are known as unisons.

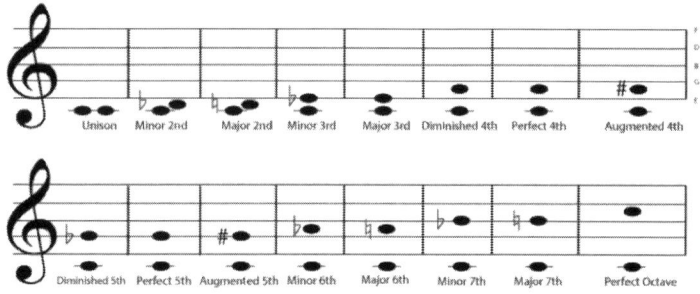

The different pitch intervals

The second part of an interval name is referred to as the prefix. The prefix is determined by the quality of the interval. There are five major prefixes that are used to describe intervals. A perfect interval is one that includes both an octave and a unison. Perfect intervals also have a fourth and a fifth. A perfect interval is labelled with the symbol 'P.' The next prefix is the major. This can only describe seconds, thirds, sixths and sevenths. A capital 'M' is used to label major intervals. Minor intervals are formed as a result of making a major interval smaller by half a step. This can be accomplished either by raising the bottom note by half a step or lowering the top note by half a step. A small 'm' is used to label a minor interval.

Another prefix that is commonly used to describe intervals is the augmented interval. This occurs when a major or perfect interval is made bigger by half a step without changing the interval number. Augmented intervals can be labeled using a capital 'A', the '+' symbol or the abbreviation 'Aug'. Finally, we have diminished intervals. These occur when a perfect or minor interval is made smaller by half a step, while maintaining its initial interval number. A small 'd', the abbreviations 'dim' or 'deg' or the symbol '°' can be used to denote a diminished interval.

From the above, it becomes evident that octaves, unisons, fourths and fifths can be either diminished, perfect or augmented. On the other hand, thirds, sixths and sevenths can be either diminished, augmented, major or minor.

Scales and Key Signatures

Musical notes are sometimes arranged in scales. A scale is a set of notes which are ordered per increasing or decreasing differences in pitch. The pitches in a scale span an octave. Scales that include both half and whole steps are known as diatonic scales. Each note within a diatonic scale has a specific name. The first and last notes in a diatonic scale are known as the tonic. Tonics are the easiest to find and the most stable. As a result, you will find that most diatonic melodies will often end with a diatonic note. The second note in the diatonic scale is known as the supertonic. The third note, which sits halfway between the tonic and the dominant is known as the mediant. After the mediant comes the subdominant, which is the fourth note in the diatonic scale. The fifth note is known as the dominant. Next to the dominant, we have the submediant. The seventh note is known as the subtonic. In the major, harmonic and melodic minor scales, if the seventh note is half a step lower than the tonic, it is referred to as the leading note.

The Major Scale

This is one of the most famous scales. This scale is made up of seven different pitches. The escalation of pitches on this scale is what is expressed by the familiar "Doh Re Mi Fa So La Ti Doh". The Major Scale has two half steps. One falls between the third and the fourth scale degrees while the other falls between the seventh and eighth scale degress. The other scale degrees are separated by whole steps. Below is an image of the C Major Scale.

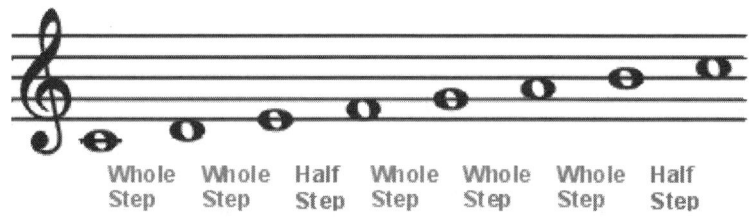

Whole and half steps in the C major scale

All major scales maintain the same pattern of whole and half steps. To construct another major scale, you only need to change the first note and then maintain the same sequence of whole and half steps.

The Natural Minor Scales

Natural minor scales consist of seven different scale degrees, with two half steps. The first half step falls between the second and third degree while the second falls between the fifth and sixth degree. The other scale degrees are separated by whole steps. Below is an image of the A minor scale. Just as with the major scales, you can construct other minor scales by changing the first note of the A minor scale and maintaining the same pattern.

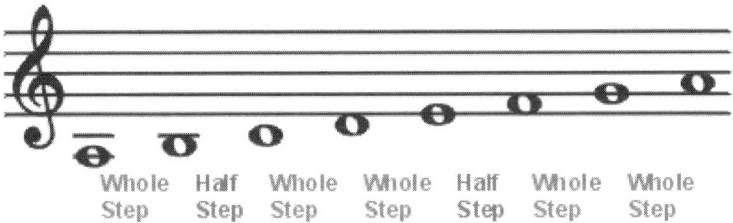

Whole and half steps in the A minor scale

The Harmonic Minor Scale

The Haromonic minor is similar to the natural minor scale. However, the seventh step of the harmonic minor scale is raised half a step. This means that the interval between the sixth and seventh notes becomes one and a half steps while the interval between the seventh and eighth notes becomes one half step. Below is an image of the harmonic A minor scale.

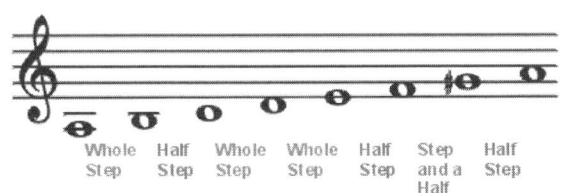

Whole, half and one and half steps in the harmonic minor scale

The Melodic Minor Scale

This is another scale that is the result of a slight variation of the natural minor scale. Here, the sixth and seventh notes are both raised by half a step. All the other notes maintain the same pattern as with the natural major scale. Below is an image of the melodic A minor scale.

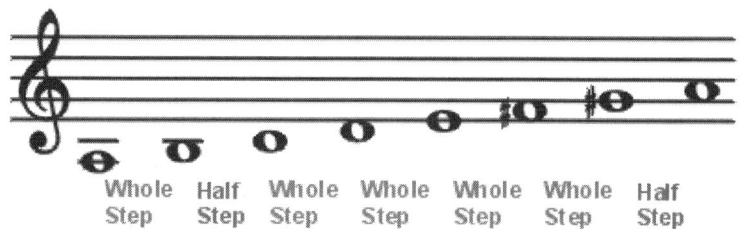

Whole and half steps on the melodic minor scale

Pentatonic Scales

As their name suggests, pentatonic scales consist of only five notes. Since they are a couple of notes less than the diatonic scales, pentatonic scales need intervals of more than half a step in order to get from one end of the scale to the other.

Some scales do not follow the interval sequences of either the diatonic or pentatonic scales. Such scales are known as nondiatonic scales. Most nondiatonic scales do not have an identifiable tonic.

An example of a well-known non-diatonic scale in Western music theory is the chromatic scale, which consists of an octave divided into twelve consecutive tones. This scale only consists of half steps. Since all the notes are equidistant, the chromatic scale does not have a tonic. Whole tone scales, on the other hand, are non-diatonic scales that are comprised of whole steps only. Whole tone scales also do not have tonics. The blues scale is another scale that is derived by adding a chromatic variation to the major scale. The blues scale has flat thirds and sevenths alternating with normal thirds and sevenths. The blues inflection occurs as a result of this alternation.

Transposition

It is possible to duplicate scale patterns at different pitches. This is known as transposition. For instance, if you write the major scale pattern but decide to start at the pitch G, the result becomes a transposition. However, you would still maintain the same pattern used by the major scale. It is possible to modify all the notes of a piece of music this way.

In some cases, however, some notes become sharp once they are transposed. In such instances, you might opt to place accidentals at the beginning of the piece. This modifies all the notes of a specific pitch. By placing the accidental at the beginning of the piece (instead of right beside the note), the accidental affects all the notes in the piece. For instance, placing a sharp at the beginning of line F makes all the Fs sharp. This designation of sharps and flats at the beginning of a piece is known as a key signature.

Key Signatures

In Western music theory, the pitches that make up a scale are designated by key signatures at the beginning of a composition. At times, the scale may shift as the music progresses. However, the interval relationships do not change even when the scale changes. To make key signatures easier to understand and remember, sometimes a chart known as the circle of fifths is used. On the outer side of this chart are the major key names. They are separated by fifths. On the inside of the chart are the minor key names. Between the two are staves showing the number and positions of the flats and sharps.

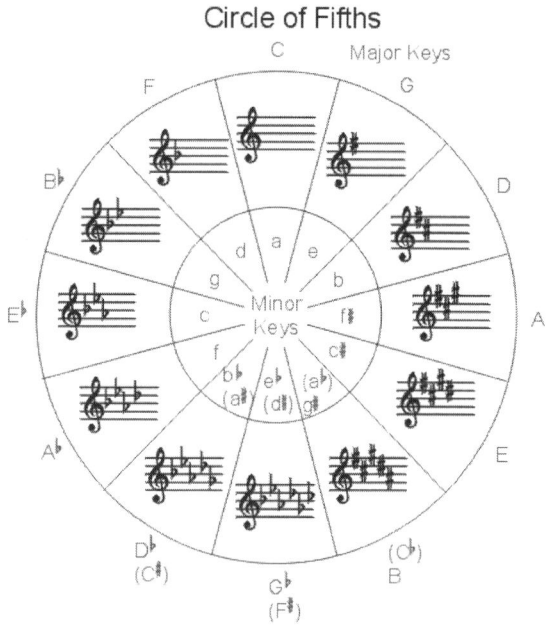

Modes

A mode refers to a type of scale that is coupled with specific melodic behaviors. Modes were developed in the middle ages as a way of organizing the melodic and harmonic parts of music. The usage of modes fell somewhat from the 17th to the 19th century. They were replaced by the major and minor scales. However, modes are still used in contemporary music. Unlike the tonic in a diatonic scale, the beginning tone of a mode is known as the final.

There are several modes. The most common is the Dorian mode, which resembles the natural minor scale with the sixth note raised. The half steps in the Dorian mode fall between the second and third and the sixth and seventh degrees. The Phrygian mode corresponds to the natural minor scale, with the second note lowered. The half steps fall between the first and second and fifth and sixth notes. The Lydian mode corresponds to the major scale, with a raised fourth note. The half steps fall between the fourth and fifth and seventh and eighth notes. The Mixolydian mode is similar to the major scale, with the seventh note lowered. The half steps fall between the third and fourth and sixth and seventh notes. The Aeolian mode is similar to the natural minor scale. Its half steps are placed between the second and third and fifth and sixth notes. The Ionian mode is similar to the major scale, with the half steps between the third and fourth and seventh and eighth notes. Finally, we have the Locrian mode, which corresponds to the natural minor, albeit with lowered second and fifth notes. The half steps on the Locrian mode fall between the first and second and fourth and fifth notes. However, Locrian modes are rarely used.

Just like scales, modes can begin on any tone, provided that the pattern of half and whole steps remains unchanged. Identifying the identity of a transposed mode is easy since its final lies in the same position as the tonic of a major with a similar key signature.

Solfeggio

Solfeggio, sometimes referred to as solfege is a voice exercise which is used to teach pitch and sight singing. The solfeggio consists of syllables which are associated to specific notes in each scale. The syllable 'Do' corresponds to the first note or the tonic. The next syllable is 'Re', which corresponds to the supertonic. The mediant is represented by the syllable 'Mi'. The subdominant is represented by the syllable 'Fa'. The dominant is represented by the syllable 'Sol'. The next syllable is 'La', which represents the submediant. Finally, we have the syllable 'Ti', which corresponds to the leading tone.

Consonance and Dissonance

This refers to the categorization of sounds that are played simultaneously or successively. Consonant notes sound pleasant, sweet and stable when played together. Dissonant notes sound unpleasant or harsh. It is important to note that consonance and dissonance are subjective. What sounds good to one person may not sound pleasant to the other. These values may also be affected by context and other aspects such as tuning. However, there are common notes that are associated with consonance or dissonance.

Consonance and dissonance applies to both intervals and chords. The octave, the major and minor third, the perfect fourth and fifth and the major and minor sixth are simple intervals that are associated with consonance. They sound pleasing when played together.

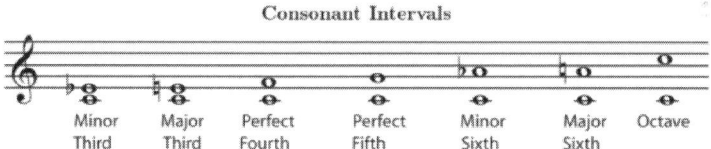

The major and minor second, the major and minor seventh and triton (the interval between the perfect fourth and fifth) are intervals associated with dissonance. They seem to clash when played together. When we hear dissonant chords, we expect them to move to a consonant chord. When a dissonance moves to a consonance, this is known as a resolution. A good pattern of dissonances and consonances is what makes music exciting.

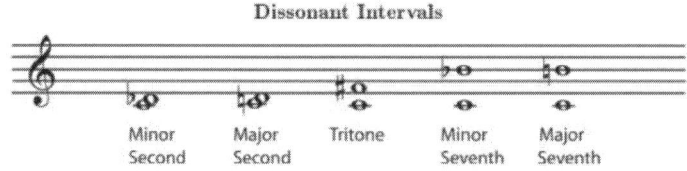

Rhythm

Rhythm in a piece of music refers to the sequential arrangement of sounds and silences as they progress through time. Rhythm can also be referred to as the basic pulse or pattern that is repeated through the progress of a piece of music. These pulses are referred to as beats. In a written piece of music, the beats are placed together in groupings known as measures or bars. In most pieces of music, the bars have an equal number of beats. The first beat in a bar usually sounds as the strongest. The bars in a piece of music set up the underlying rhythm of the music.

Melody

This is one of the foundational elements of music theory. A melody is a series of notes of a particular pitch and duration, stringed together to form a succession that typically escalates towards a crescendo of tension before resolving to a state of rest. However, a melody is more than a series of notes. A melody is the part of music that catches your ear. The basic elements that comprise a melody are the pitch, rhythm, duration and tempo of the string of notes.

There are some other important terms that are used to describe melody. The series of notes that make up a melody are known as the melodic line. Ornaments or embellishments refer to notes that the composer or performer adds to make a melody exciting and complex.

They are not part of the main melodic line. They only serve to enhance the melody.

Melody affects how music sounds. A melody usually involves changes in pitch as it progresses to keep the music interesting. A melody that progresses on one pitch will quickly become boring. The rise and fall of the pitch of a melody written on the staff creates a line that rises and falls. This line is referred to as the shape or contour of the melodic line.

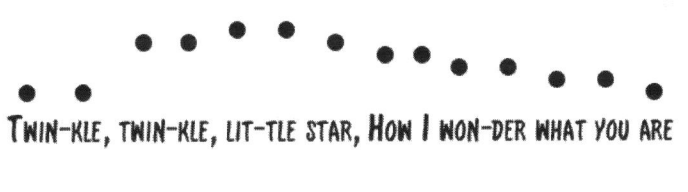

Melodic contour of a popular musical composition

Chord

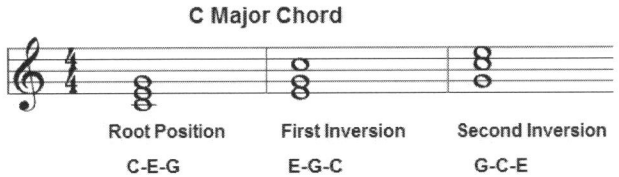

In music theory, a chord is a set of three or more harmonic notes that sound as if they are played simultaneously. They don't need to actually be played together. Chords and sequences of chords (ordered sequences of chords, also known as chord progressions) are common in most kinds of modern Western, Oceanian and West African music. However, they are lacking in music from most other parts of the world.

The most common kind of chords are known as triads. Triads are made up of three distinct notes – the root note and two intervals of a third and fifth directly on top of the root note. More notes can be added to triads to form other kinds of chords like the extended chords, seventh cords or added tone chords. The most common chords include the minor and major triads and the augmented and diminished triads. The phrases minor, major, diminished and augmented are sometimes used to refer to the quality of the chord. The root note is usually used to classify chords. For instance, a major chord that is rooted on the note C is classified as chord C major.

Harmony

Harmony is another one of the key tenets of music theory. Harmony occurs in music when more than one pitches, tones, notes or chords are sounded at the same time. Harmony refers to how the tones and chords accompanying a melody interplay together to add meaning and depth to music. In music, harmony does have to actually sound "harmonious". The essence of harmony of the notes, pitches and chords sounding simultaneously. In some cases, harmony may actually be dissonant.

Harmonies in music come in different textures. When a melody is composed such that it strongly suggests a harmony that could go together with it – even without any other notes sounding simultaneously – is known as **implied harmony**. The easiest way of adding harmony to a melody is by playing it alongside **drones**. These are notes that do not change throughout the course of a musical piece. When different lines in a piece of music rise and fall together in accordance with the melody, this is known as **parallel harmony**. When a piece of music has one distinct melodic line while the rest of the notes are included simply to add harmony, this is known as **homophony**. When a piece of music has more than one independent and fairly equal melodic lines, this is known as **polyphony** or a **counterpoint**.

Timbre

Sometimes referred to as "color", this refers to the differences in musical sound resulting from the instrument used to play the sound. This is what enables us to distinguish between two different instruments. For instance, if a flute and recorder play the same note at the same pitch and volume, you can distinguish between the sounds from the two instruments. This difference between the two sounds is what is known as timbre.

The differences in timber between different instruments arises from the fact that each instrument produces sounds in a complex wave that has more than one frequency. As humans, we do not hear these different frequencies as separate notes. Instead, we hear them as a mixture of frequencies that form the color of the sound. In addition, the timbre of an instrument can be altered by employing different playing techniques.

Humans are capable of perceiving and appreciating very minute differences in the timbre of musical sounds. Not only can a person tell the difference between two instruments, they can also distinguish between two instruments of the same kind.

There are many different words used to describe various forms of timbre. Some of these words are interchangeable and have no specific definitions. Some of these include dull, clear, bright, rounded, harsh, mellow, warm, reedy, dark, shrill, piercing, brassy, strident, and so on.

Dynamics

In music, dynamics refers to how loud or quiet a performance is. While the volume of a musical performance can be accurately measured by audio engineers, dynamics are not given any absolute values in music notation. Instead, dynamics are considered as relative values. Since dynamics are a subjective value, the volume of a performance is determined by several factors aside from amplitude, including factors like timer and articulation.

In a written piece of music, dynamics are represented by symbols or abbreviations which show the volume at which different notes should be played. These symbols are derived from the Italian language and are used to indicate the different parts that require different volumes in the same way punctuation is used in a sentence.

Below are some of the symbols used to represent various levels intensity, together with their actual Italian and English meanings.

Abbreviation	Italian word	English meaning
ppp	Pianissisamo	Very, very quiet
pp	Pianissimo	Very quiet
mp	Mezzopiano	Quite quiet
p	Piano	Quiet
f	Forte	Loud
mf	Mezzoforte	Quite loud
ff	Fortissimo	Very loud
fff	Fortississimo	Very, very loud
sf	Sforzando	Suddenly very loud
cres.	Cresendo	Getting louder
dim.	Diminuendo	Getting quieter

Articulation

In music, articulation refers to the performer's style and how it impacts the length or duration of a series of notes in relation to each other. Articulation is not quantified. Instead, it is only described, giving the performer room to interpret how to execute the articulation.

Articulation marks are used to express articulations. These articulation marks establish a relationship between the notes in a piece of music and modify their execution.

Some common articulation marks used in music include the staccato, staccatissimo, marcato, legato, slur, detache, rinforzando and sforzando. There are symbols that are used above articulation marks to specify the type of articulation. For instance, a dot is used to indicate a staccato while a curved line connecting two or more notes indicates a slur.

Most types of articulations can be fitted into one of three general categories. Some articulations represent **dynamic change**. These show the need for a change in volume in relation to surrounding notes. The sforzando and marcato are examples of articulations that represent dynamic change. Articulations like the tenuto, staccato and staccatissimo represent **length change**. They are used to elongate or shorten notes. While every articulation changes a note in relation to the notes around it, some articulations affect a group of notes as a whole. These articulations represent **relationship change**. Examples of articulations that represent relationship change are the slur and detache.

Texture

The texture of a piece of music refers to how the composer combines the melody, rhythm and harmony to bring out the general quality of the piece. Put simply, texture describes how complex a musical composition is, or how different layers or elements are used in the piece to create a musical "tapestry." Texture is very often a relative term, though it can also be distinguished specifically depending on the number of elements in the compositions and how they relate to each other. Texture is affected by tempo, harmony and rhythm of a piece, the amount and richness of instruments used to play the piece as well as the timbre of these instruments.

The following terms are commonly used to describe texture:

Monophonic: This is a composition has a single melodic line. There's no harmony or counterpoint.

Biphonic: Biphonic music has two different melodies that play simultaneously.

Heterophonic: Consists of a single melody, with different variations of this melody being played or sung simultaneously.

Homophonic: Music that has a single melodic line with chords or accompaniment.

Polyphonic: This is a piece of music that has several harmonies and voices.

Form or Structure

Form refers to the overall plan or structure of a piece of music. In other words, form looks at the big picture in a piece of music. There is a great range of complexity in musical form. While most listeners will quickly understand the form of short, simple pieces of music, it can be difficult to understand the form of more complex or unfamiliar types of music. A person can still enjoy a piece of music without having to recognize its form. However, seeing the "big picture" makes the music even more enjoyable for the listener.

Musical form can be described by labelling it with letters or giving names to the very common forms. For instance, the first major section in the piece of music can be labelled A. If another section is exactly similar to the first section, it also gets labelled A. If it is quite similar but has some distinct differences, it could be labelled A' (A prime). Another distinct variation of A could be labelled A" (A double prime).

Expression

Musical expression refers to the art of expressing emotion through music and invoking emotions from the audience. Expression thus forms an emotional link between the performer and the audience. Musical expression explores how a performer brings a piece of music to life through the appropriate use of dynamics, articulation, phrasing, intensity, timbre, energy and excitement. The aim of musical expression is to elicit responses from the audience. Through a piece of music, the performer can calm or excite the audience and affect their physical and emotional responses in other ways.

Musical expression is not the result of a single element. Instead, it is the result of a combination of several musical elements used simultaneously. Musical expression also depends on the natural ability of the performer to express deep emotions and sentiment.

Notation

Musical notation refers to the symbolized or written representation of a piece of music. Music is represented in written form through the use of generally accepted graphic symbols as well as written instructions and their abbreviations. Different cultures and different ages use different systems of music notation. The Western notation in use today evolved during the middle ages. To this day, it is still undergoing various forms of experimentation and innovation. Sometimes, hand signs and spoken language can also be used to represent music. However, these are mostly used in teaching.

Western music notation uses symbols (notes) placed on a musical staff to graphically represent tones. There are different symbols for representing other musical elements like dynamics, articulations. Duration, keys, rests, accents, etc. The conductor usually uses verbal instructions to indicate aspects like technique and tempo.

Common Practice Part Writing

Common-practice part writing is a very crucial skill in music theory. While modern musical law does not incorporate practice-writing, knowing the rules on which practice writing is based can be very advantageous in analyzing and understanding music. Common practice has its foundations on the rules of counterpoint. This is a set of rules which were very popular in the 18th and 19th centuries. The aim of counterpoint was to come up with harmonies and progressions that people from that era found enjoyable and acceptable. Counterpoint was used by famous musicians like Beethoven, Brahms, Mozart, Handel and Bach. Music written in this style is often divided into two parts, each with four different species: 1st, 2nd, 3rd and 4th. Each of these parts defines a different way that the part interacts with different rhythms.

Common practice part writing is best represented in four-part writing, the most common of which is the chorale style which uses two voice parts per clef. The chorale style is based around bass, tenor, alto and soprano voices. The tenor and bass voices are written on the bass clef while the soprano and alto voices are written on the treble clef. The four different voices are then used together to come up with chordal progressions. There are several different rules which are used to define the movement of chordal progressions.

When writing a piece of music, the composer must concentrate on the spacing and range of each instrument or voice. It is very important for the composer not to stretch the range of an instrument higher or lower than it is usually used to. They must also be very careful of spacing, since wrong spacing can lead to voice crossing. This is where a voice or instrument goes higher or lower than the voice that is above or below it. Common-practice part writing strictly forbids voice crossing. For instance, the soprano voice is not supposed to go lower than the alto voice.

When part writing, it is important to use the Conjunct Melodic Motion, where the different parts generally move in stepwise motion. If you are using counterpoint, if a part jumps to a fourth or above, it should then progress in stepwise motion in the direction opposite the jump. The different voices are also required to progress together in contrary motion, which means that each voice goes in a different direction. This is preferable to having the voices move together in parallel motion, or having one voice move while the other doesn't, as in oblique motion.

In cases where the composer decides to use parallel motion, they must pay special attention to the intervals to ensure that they are in line with the counterpoint rules. Dissonant intervals should be avoided, whether they are melodic or harmonic. This includes seventh chords, tritons and diminished or augmented intervals. Using these intervals results in a jarring piece of music. The composer should also be aware of parallel intervals. These occur when two voices move the same distance, resulting in a similar interval twice in a row. However, this is not always a problem, unless the intervals are a perfect octave or perfect fifth, in which case the piece has a hollow or open sound which is a bit uncomfortable to the ear.

Chapter Two: Fundamentals of Music Notation

People invented language long before they learned how to write. Similarly, people started making music long before they came up with a system of writing down music. Before the advent of written music, people played music by the ear. To this day, some musicians still play music this way. However, written music has a number of advantages. It is much easier to study and share. Written music also makes it possible for bands and large groups of musicians to play long, complex pieces exactly as the composer intended. While there are many different types of music notation in existence, the most common and most popular is the use of the staff.

The Staff

The staff (plural staves) is the backbone of written music. It provides a backdrop on which musical symbols are placed. The staff is made up of five horizontal parallel lines and the four spaces between them. Below is an image of a simple unadorned staff.

An unadorned staff

    Musical notations are placed on the staff, either on the lines or in the spaces between them. The notation of music on the staff is very logical. The higher a note is on the staff, the higher the pitch of the note. The lower the note on the staff, the lower the pitch. Sometimes, a note may have an extreme pitch that goes beyond the staff, either too high or too low. In this case, ledger lines are used to temporarily extend the staff vertically to accommodate these notes. You can think of a staff like the two dimensional mathematical plane, with the Y-axis representing pitch while the X-axis represents time.

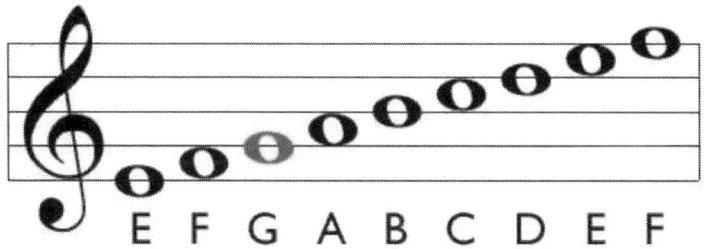

Staff adorned with notes

    The notes and rests appearing on the staff are the actual written music. Notes represent sounds while rests represent silence. Vertical lines known as bar lines are used to divide the staff into short sections referred to as bars or measures, while double bar lines are used to signify the end of larger sections or even the end of a piece of music. Important symbols like clefs and time and key and time signatures are placed at the beginning of the staff. Other symbols are placed above the music to direct how other elements of the music should be executed.

Evolution of Staff Notation

The notation of musical notes and symbols on the modern staff evolved from the neumatic notations which was used between the 9th and 12th centuries for secular song and plainchant. Neumes were graphical symbols which were essentially used to indicate the rise and fall of the voice. Neumes themselves evolved from Greek and Roman symbols which were used to guide declamation. Different regions had different musical adaptations of these symbols. Unlike modern musical symbols, each neume consisted of two or more notes, with indications of their approximate relative pitches. The notes within a single syllable of text were represented using a single neume.

Unlike modern staff notation, neumes only acted as memory aids to singers who already knew a piece of music by heart. A singer who had no prior knowledge of the words and melody of a piece and music could not sing it by reading neumes. However, between the 10th and 12th centuries, there were significant developments towards a notation system that could allow people to sight-read music. 'Distematic' neumes, also known as 'heighted' neumes were used with varying spaces relative to each other, forming a continuous graph of pitch above the words of a piece of music.

Eventually, to make the pitch more precise, people started spacing the neumes on a horizontal grid of scratched lines. The degrees of a scale would then fall alternatively on a line or space in similar fashion to the modern staff. One line on the grid was colored red to represent the pitch F and another was colored yellow to represent pitch C. Eventually, the letters F or C started being used at the beginning of the appropriate lines to represent these pitches. By the 13th century, a four line staff was widely in use, with stylized forms of the letters F, C and G acting as clefs. By the 14th century, the five line staff had become the standard for polyphonic music.

In the 12th century, musicians in northern and north eastern France started adding more thickness to the thin, curved lines of neumes at specific points to define the separate notes within the neumes. This led to the rise of groupings of notes known as ligatures. Later, the ligatures were used to represent polyphonies which were without text. No longer tied to syllabic considerations, the ligatures attained rhythmic significance. However, the meaning of the ligatures still depending on context. In the 13th century, time values were codified for the ligatures, single notes and rests.

These new symbols with codified time values would form the basis for the mensural notation, which was popular between the 13th to 15th centuries. In the mensural notation system, the value of a note was determined relative to the value of its neighbors, based on several fundamental principles that were the basis of this system. This system would later evolve into the modern staff notation beginning in the 16th century. Longer note values became obsolete and shorter ones were introduced. The use of bar lines to measure meter, which had started in the late 15th century, became part of staff notation in the 17th century. Other aspects like regularly spaced barring and separate tempo indications become part of staff notation in the 18th and 19th centuries.

Groups of Staves

Just like normal text, music on the staff is read from left to right. Therefore, the notes to the left are played before those to the right. From the top of the page, each staff is read on its own, unless there is a group of connected staff. Connected staves should be played simultaneously. They are usually connected by a long vertical line on the left hand side. In other cases, bar lines may be used to connect staves. If a group of staves should be played by similar instruments or the same person, braces or brackets are used to group these staves together.

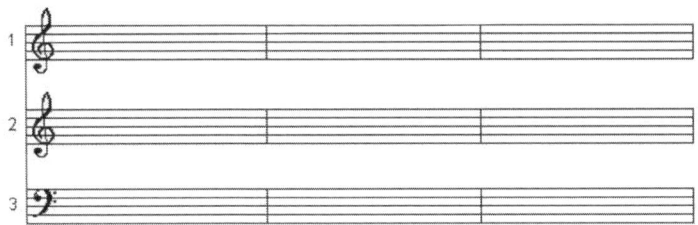

The Grand Staff

The grand staff is a combination of the bass and treble clef, connected together by a brace and line. This allows for notation of a wide range of pitches. The grand staff is commonly used in playing piano music, since it can accommodate the piano's wide range. It tells exactly which key should be played when.

Clefs

Clefs are the fancy symbols that appear at the beginning of each music staff. The clef symbol is used to associate the lines and spaces of the staff with particular pitches. There are many clefs in existence, many of which were used in the past. Today, only a couple of clefs are still used regularly. These are:

The Treble Clef

The treble clef, also known as the G-clef, is the most common clef in written music. It marks a treble sound. The treble clef, which is shaped like a stylized G, coils around the second the second lowermost line on the staff. It marks this line to be a G. From that, one can come up with the arrangement of the next letters on the staff. Each next letter is placed on a higher space or line. You should also note that the letter G is followed by an A. The lines on a treble staff in ascending order are E, G, B, D, F. You can use the following mnemonic to remember them: Every Good Boy Deserves Fudge. The spaces in ascending order are F, A, C, E, spelling the word FACE.

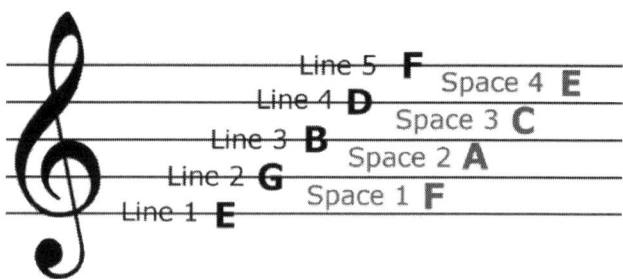

The Bass Clef

The bass clef is also known as the F clef. This clef designates the note F as the line bracketed by the two dots on the F-clef symbol. From there, one can identify the rest of the notes, which are still arranged in ascending order. This F-clef staff is usually used for low-pitched instruments. The lines on the bass staff, in ascending order are G, B, D, F, A. To remember the names of the lines on a bass staff, use the mnemonic "Good Boys Don't Fool Around". The spaces on this staff are A, C, E, and G. The spaces can be remembered using the following mnemonic: All Cows Eat Grass.

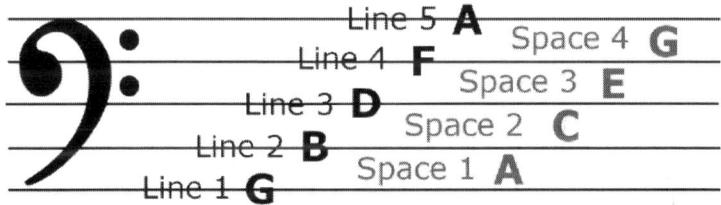

The C-Clef

Another clef that was popular is the C-clef, though its use is very infrequent nowadays. The C-clef is a movable clef. It can be placed anywhere on the staff. It has different names depending on its position on the staff. Depending on what line it is on, it is given names like the Alto Clef, the Tenor Clef, the Baritone Clef, the Soprano Clef or the Mezzo Soprano Clef. Regardless of its position, the line on which the C-Clef centers represents a middle C.

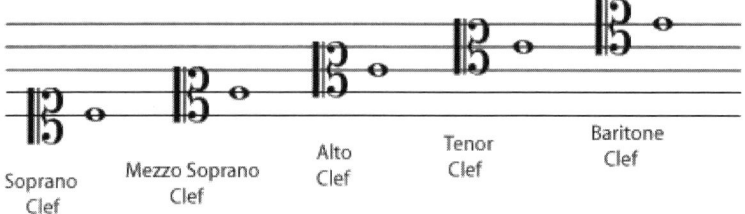

Measures

Measures, also known as bars, are marked by the vertical lines on the staff. They are used to organize music into sections. The number of beats in a measure is determined by the time signature. The beginning and end of a piece of music are marked using thick double bars. Sometimes, numbers are used to mark measures for easier navigation.

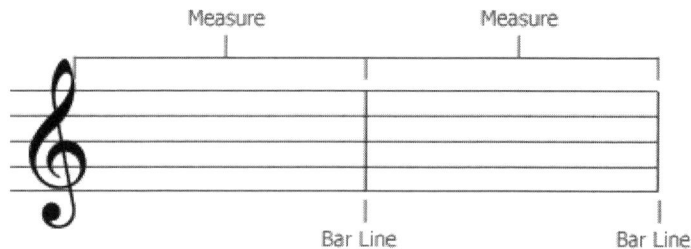

Notes

Notes are used to represent pitches on the staff, with letters being used to distinguish between the different pitches. The letters used to name pitches, in ascending order, are A, B, C, D, E, E, F and G. After G, the cycle starts again at A. The different lines of the staff represent different pitches, with lower lines representing low pitches and higher lines representing higher pitches. A note is represented on the staff using a small oval symbol.

Notes on the Staff

Notes are either placed on the lines or within the spaces on the staff. For notes with stems, the stems are placed on the left side of the note trailing down if the note is above the middle line. For those below the middle line, the stem rises upwards from the right side of the note. For notes on the middle line, the stem usually goes down, unless there are adjacent notes with flags that go up. The stems are usually one octave long (4 lines and 4 spaces). In case there are two melodies on the same staff, the stems for notes of one melody point up while those of the other melody point down.

Ledger Lines

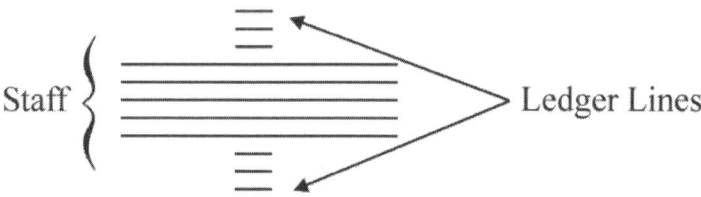

Ledger lines are lines that extend the vertical length of the staff, allowing for notes with higher or lower pitches than the staff to still be shown on the staff. The naming of ledger lines follows the same pattern used for the lines of the staff. The stems of notes placed on ledger lines point towards the center of the staff.

Note Durations

Each note has a specific duration.

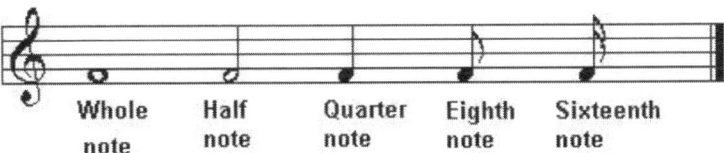

The largest note value is the whole note. A whole note has double the duration of a half note. Similarly, a half note has double the length of a quarter note, while a quarter note has double the length of an eighth note. An eighth note has double the length of a sixteenth note. This hierarchy can continue to infinity, with an addition of flags as the note is broken down into smaller units.

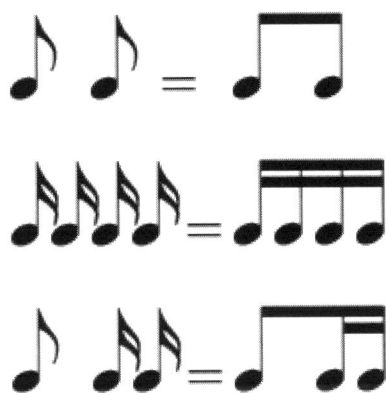

Two sixteenth or eighth notes can also be combined to look like the above image. Since eighth and sixteenth notes have flags, when they combine the flags are turned into connecting bars. An eighth and a sixteenth may also be combined.

Dotted Notes

Dots may be used besides notes. They increase the length of a note by half its original length. For instance, if a half note was worth 2 beats, placing a dot next to it makes it worth three beats.

Rests

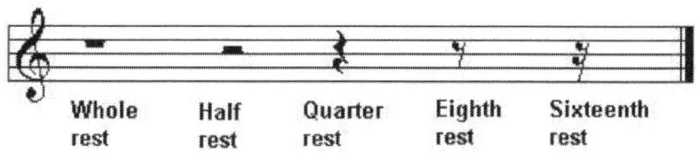

Whole rest   Half rest   Quarter rest   Eighth rest   Sixteenth rest

Rests are periods of silence where the musician does not play any note. Rests are given values that correspond to those of notes. Therefore, just like notes, there are whole rests, half rests, quarter rests and so on. Unlike notes which change their vertical position depending on the pitch, rests always maintain the same vertical position.

Accidentals

Accidentals are used to modify the pitch of a note. They do this by either decreasing or increasing the pitch by half a step. Once an accidental appears on the staff, it affects all the notes of equivalent pitch for the remaining part of the measure. However, when they appear at the very beginning of a piece of music, accidentals are used to specify key signature.

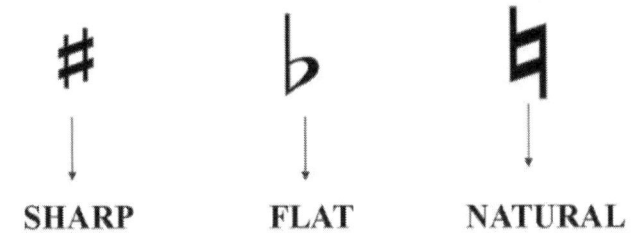

There are three types of accidental symbols. Flats are used to take the pitch of a note a half step lower. Sharps are used to raise the pitch of a note a half step higher, while naturals cancel out any previous accidentals. When a natural appears, the pitch goes back to normal.

Ties and Slurs

Ties and slurs are used to link together two or more notes. Ties link together notes of the same pitch to create a single but longer note. Slurs, on the other hand, link together notes of different pitches. In effect, this means that these notes should be played without any break between them.

Repeats

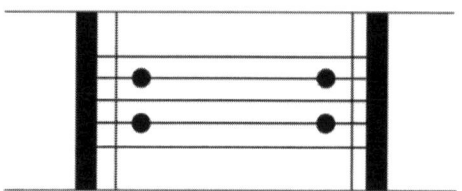

The above symbols are used to show the beginning and end of a repeat. When you come across the second repeat sign, it means that you should go back and repeat the music from the point where the first repeat sign appeared. Repeat signs usually go hand in hand with endings.

D.S.

This stands for 'Del Signo'. It is a directional marking. When this appears in a piece of music, it directs the player to go to the sign (Shown below). The Del Signo symbol usually goes hand in hand with an 'al coda' or al fine'. When accompanied by 'al coda', it means that you should 'Go to the sign, from there go to the coda'. If accompanied by an 'al fine', it means 'Go to the sign, from there go to the end'.

This is the sign that was referred to above. From here, the music should be plated to the coda or wherever the Del Signo indicates.

The above sign represents the coda. It shows instances where the player is supposed to go to the special ending, also known as the coda.

Time Signatures

These are also known as meter signatures. They tell the player the number of beats in a measure and the notes that get the beat.

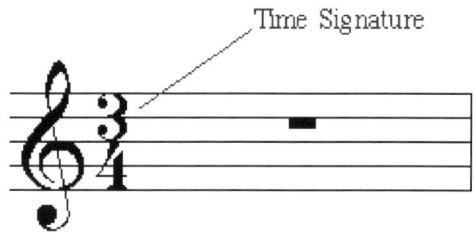

The top number in the time signature shows the number of beats in the measure. The bottom number, on the other hand, determines the note that gets the beat. For instance, when the time signature is 3/4, it means that each measure has 3 beats, while the beat goes to the fourth note.

Chapter Three: Elements of Reading Sheet Music

Sheet music refers to music where the different musical aspects of the composition – pitches, chords, rhythms, melodies, etc. – are represented in handwritten or printed form using modern musical symbols placed on a staff. Sheet music has different parts, comes in different types and is written for different purposes and uses.

Title And Credit

The first thing in a piece of music is the title of the song or composition. In most modern forms of sheet music, the title of the composition is indicated on the cover or title page. If there is no cover or title page, the title is indicated at the top of the first page. If the composition or song is taken from a bigger work such as a movie or opera, the title of the main work is also indicated. The name of the songwriter or composer is usually written along with the title of the composition. If the songwriter is unknown, this can be left out. If the lyrics of the song are written by a different person, the name of the lyric-writer may also be included. This is the same case for the name of the arranger. If the composition is an old folk music, a traditional hymn or spiritual or if it belongs to traditional genres such as blues, the name of the composer or songwriter is usually left out. This is because most of these songs have no known authors. For such pieces, the word "Traditional" is often used instead of the composer's name.

After the title and credit comes the actual written music, the elements of which were discussed in detail in the previous chapter.

Purpose and Use of Sheet Music

Sheet music is written for one of the following three reasons:

- To act as a record of music
- To act as a guide to a piece of music
- To provide the means for performing a piece of music.

To understand sheet music, one needs to be able to read music notation, which we discussed earlier. However, one does not need to be able to read or write music in order to compose music. Several famous songwriters and composers – the likes of Paul McCartney, John Stanley and Lionel Bert – have produced great music without being able to read music.

A popular skill when it comes to reading sheet music is sight reading. This is the ability of a person to perform a piece of music after viewing it for the first time, without prior practice. Most professional musicians are expected to be well skilled in sight reading. Some more experienced musicians can even hear all the sounds in a piece of music in their head after looking at it for the first time, without even having to hear the piece being played.

Sheet music is very important when it comes to performing some forms of music, such as chamber music, orchestral works, singing choral works and sonatas. The musicians performing these kinds of music usually have the sheet music on a music stand in front of them. However, musicians performing solo pieces do not usually read from sheet music. Instead, they are expected to memorize the music. Jazz music also uses an improvised form of sheet music known as a lead sheet to give indications of the different elements of the music.

Traditional forms of music rarely depend on sheet music. Instead, traditional musicians usually learn how to play music by the ear, or by being taught by another person. While sheet music often serves as a platform for new music and helps in the composition of new music, it can also act as a visual record of existing music.

Types of Sheet Music

Written music comes in different types. If a composition is meant to be played using only one instrument or voice, it is usually written as a single piece of sheet music. In other cases, a piece may be intended to be performed by different persons. In this case, each performer will have a different piece of the sheet music, which is known as a part.

Sometimes, separate vocal and instrumental parts of a piece of music may be written together, resulting in what is known as a score. There are various formats of musical scores:

Full score: This refers to a large book that shows the parts of the instruments and voices in a piece of music. Full scores are mainly used by conductors to lead an ensemble. They may also be used as a basis for studying a given work of music.

Miniature score: This is a smaller version of a full score. For this reason, it cannot be used by a conductor. However, it is still a handy tool for those looking to study a piece of music.

Study score: Study scores are sometimes similar in size and can be difficult to distinguish from miniature scores. However, study scores may include comments about the music for study purposes.

Piano score: This is a piece of sheet music that has been simplified or compressed such that it can fit on the grand staff and is therefore playable by piano. Reducing a score into a piano score takes considerable skill, since the score needs to be detailed enough to present all the elements of the composition while still remaining playable on the piano.

Vocal score: This is a full score that has been reduced to only show the vocal parts on their staves. Vocal scores make it easy and convenient for vocal performers to learn and rehearse music separately.

While these are the main types of scores, there are other minor types of scores, such as:

Short scores: These refer to scores that take a piece of music meant for many instruments and compress it to just a few staves. Short scores are typically used when composing music, then get expanded later to complete the orchestration.

Open score: This is a piece that places each voice on its own staff.

Chapter Four: Seven Step-by-Step Exercises to Help You Learn How to Read Sheet Music

Having learnt the basics of music theory, the fundamentals of music notation and the elements of sheet music, now is the time to put your knowledge into practice. Like with learning any other language, learning how to read sheet music needs lots of practice. Below is a list of step by step exercises that will speed up your learning process

Step One: Practice Full Concentration

While this may seem very obvious, it has a huge impact on your success in reading sheet music. However, without full concentration, you will easily miss notes, fly over accidentals, mess up rhythms and make a ton of other mistakes. If you are a beginner, this can be very frustrating and may even cause you to give up. Often, while trying to read a piece of music, you may find yourself reading with only half your concentration. The worst part is you might not even realize it. It's important that when you start practicing, you should clear your mind of any other distractions and focus wholly on the task at hand. The key to maintaining total concentration is to challenge yourself to complete reading an entire piece of sheet music perfectly. Try and avoid making mistakes as much as you can. If you find your mind wandering, refocus and start all over again.

Step Two: Start with Elementary Material

When starting to learn how to read sheet music, some students are often too ambitious and choose to start by reading complex musical pieces. This is not a very good approach. When learning a new language, a student starts by reading short material with simple phrases they can understand easily. As their expertise in the language grow, they graduate to reading more complex literature in the language. Similarly, you cannot learn by reading complex pieces of music. Starting with short, simple compositions allows you to acquire habits of fluency. As you get better, gradually step up the difficulty and complexity of you read. The best way to do this is to consult a qualified music teacher who can continually assess your level of knowledge and recommend suitable material.

Step Three: Divide the Music Into Chunks

During their first attempts at reading sheet music, many students try to read the music singularly. They count every single beat and take note of every single rhythm. Doing this can be very exhausting and is outright impossible. Your brain is hardwired to divide things into groups for easier comprehension. For instance, as you read this book, you are not focusing on every single letter. Instead, your brain groups letters into words and reads them as a whole. You should do the same when it comes to reading sheet music.

A good way of practicing how to read music in chunks is to divide each bar into two parts and take note of where the downbeats fall. This allows you to interpret music in a more relaxed manner and free up your mind to focus on other aspects of the piece you are reading. This also allows you to learn how to "hear" a melody by just looking at it.

Step Four: Look for Familiar Rhythms and Patterns

Each piece of music is unique different from another. However, there are certain repeated patterns that are common in many pieces of music. Some common scale fragments are found in many musical scores. These are a great start for learning how to recognize patterns in larger music sections. Try and identify different melodic lines in the music that contain ascending or descending scale fragments. Just like children have to read multiple books to get improve their word reading skills, you should also read multiple pieces of music and strive to identify the common patterns in each. You can find practice pieces online or ask a music teacher to provide you with some.

Step Five: Practice Looking Ahead

One of the main reasons that students make mistakes when reading sheet music is the simple fact that they are not ready for the upcoming notes and are hence caught off guard. A student encounters a measure that they are supposed to play immediately and they are unable to process all this information quickly. This causes them to falter as they have to think of what is required of them at that point. Such a pause ruins the flow of the whole piece of music. To avoid being caught off guard, students should get into the practice of continuously scanning ahead to be aware of the notes and rhythms coming up. Always scan a beat or two ahead of whatever you are currently playing. This skill requires you to use a combination of all the other skills mentioned above. You have to focus fully on reading the music, divide the music into chunks and look for familiar patterns. All these allow you to be aware of whatever is coming up ahead.

Step Six: Learn to Continue Through Mistakes

As you learn how to read sheet music, it is inevitable that you are going to make some mistakes here and there. While you should aim for perfection, you should accept that you are going to make some mistakes. However, you should not let mistakes deter you. The most important thing is to always keep the tempo of the piece in mind, since this is what holds the whole music together. You might miss a note or an accidental, but just keep going and get the flow of the whole piece. Once you are done, restart the whole piece and try to eliminate the mistakes this time round.

Step Seven: Keep a Practice Journal

Like I noted earlier, the secret to becoming good at reading sheet music is practice. You should practice as many times as you can. This helps you to increase your skills and helps you build confidence in your skills. Ideally, you should practice reading sheet music at least 20 – 30 minutes each day. Each day, note down how long you spent practicing and what you practiced. Apart from practicing on your own, try to get together will friends or colleagues and practice together. This will help you improve your skills and increase your motivation.

Conclusion

The ability to read sheet music is a great skill to have. While learning how to read sheet music is a somewhat challenging task, it is something that one can teach themselves. All it requires is concentration, attention to details and lots of practice. I can't emphasize this enough. Practice is what will make you a skilled sheet music reader. As you get better, you will adopt to your own ways of reading music. This book has provided you with the fundamentals of music theory and music notation. It has also given you a basic introduction to sheet music and seven step by step exercises you can use to improve your sheet reading skills.

BOOK 2
HOW TO PLAY PIANO: IN 1 DAY

The Only 7 Exercises You Need to Learn Piano Theory, Piano Technique and Piano Sheet Music Today

Preston Hoffman

Table of Contents

Introduction 69

Chapter One: The Keyboard and Keys 71

Chapter Two: The Pedals 77

Chapter Three: Reading Sheet Music 81

Chapter Four: Practising Scales.. 95

Chapter Five: Adding in Chords 102

Chapter Six: Sharps and Flats.. 114

Chapter Seven: It's All About the Timing 118

Final Words 135

© Copyright 2017 - All rights reserved.

It is not legal to reproduce, duplicate, or transmit any part of this document by either electronic means or in printed format. Recording of this publication is strictly prohibited.

Introduction

Have you always wanted to learn to play the piano? Have you been hesitant about doing so because of the thought of having to spend endless hours practicing? Maybe you took some lessons but gave up because it was too hard.

What if there was a much easier way? What if I were to tell you that you could learn all the basics in seven simple lessons and that you could learn to play a proper tune in less than a day?

Does that sound a little too good to be true? Here are a couple more facts for you – playing the piano is not that complicated. It's just that the way that we are traditionally taught to play is a lot more complicated than it needs to be. Normally, you have to start by learning one note at a time, and have to learn all the theory before you get to actually start practicing what you have learned.

There is a lot of work to do before you even get close to seeing real results and that can be very disheartening.

What we do in this book is to break it down for you into simple but essential steps. You will learn the basics of music theory quickly and easily and will be able to play your first tune within hours. This will give you the motivation to carry on and keep practicing.

Will this book turn you into a maestro? No, but then it is not designed to do that. It will, however, get you started and teach you the foundations that you can build on.

You'll get to show your friends and family just how smart you are by being able to play your favorite songs – and save yourself a bundle in sheet music too.

If you are looking for an excellent introduction to playing the piano, this is the book for you. If you decide to carry on learning from there, this gives you a solid base to do that as well.

Chapter One: The Keyboard and Keys

In this chapter, you will learn about all the keys on the keyboard. This is the first step in our seven-point plan to teach you how to play the piano.

Your piano keyboard will look like this:

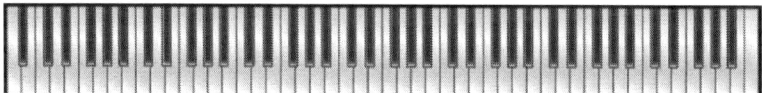

Looking down at the keyboard for the first time can be a bit intimidating. The keyboard is made up of a set of 52 white long keys, and a set of 36 shorter, more raised black keys. You should have 88 keys in total. (Some older pianos have smaller keyboards.)

Have a look at the diagram below – it is a smaller section of the keyboard, and contains all the basic information that you need to know. Once you get to know this information, you can basically apply it to the rest of the keyboard.

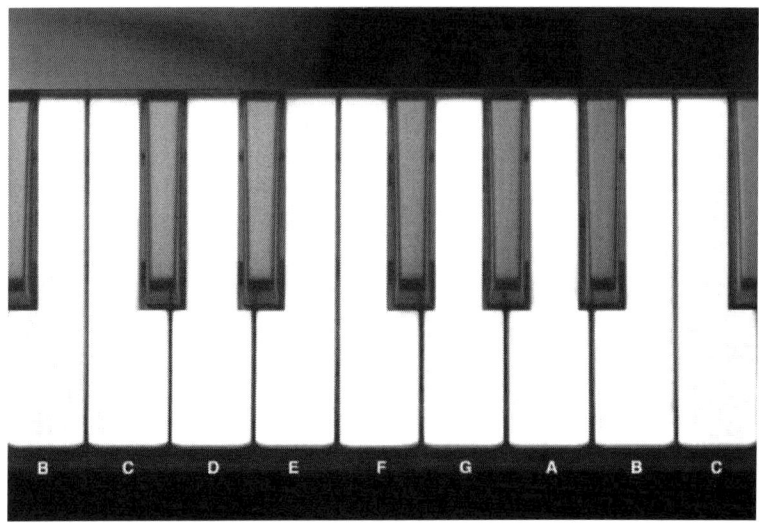

The White Keys

The white keys, as shown above, each play a particular note in music. These are named for the first seven letters of the alphabet – A through to G. There are a lot more keys than there are notes, so the letters are repeated over and over again. So, starting at the very left edge of the keyboard, you start with the letter A. The repetition makes it a lot easier – there are the same seven notes over and over again.

The next key represents the "B" chord, and so on, until you get to the key after the "G" chord. Then the keys start at "A" again. Each set represents one octave.

So, do you have to sit down and count each key from the start to determine which letter it represents?

Fortunately, there is an easier way, and that is part of the reason that we have the black keys.

The black keys are divided into groupings of twos (twins) – marked in green on the diagram above or threes (triplets) – marked in red on the diagram above. The "C" note is always to the left of a set of twins. The "F" note is always to the left of a set of the triplets. To remember this more easily, you can think of the "C" as having two points to it and the "F" as having three points to it. From there, it is easy enough to fill in the remaining letters.

Whereabouts the keys are positioned on the board indicates how high or low the note is. The lowest notes are on the left, and you move up the scales as you move over to the right.

Quick Exercise: Play each key now and see how different they all sound. Find each of the "C" keys on the keyboard. Follow with all of the "D" keys and so on. Then play the following notes on any set of the keys:

B, D, B, E, D, B.

Do you recognize the tune at all? Does it remind you of when you were a kid? It should – it's the start of "It's Raining, It's Pouring." Well done, you have just played a tune without a single music sheet in sight. Didn't I tell you that this was going to be easy?

Play it again in a different octave so that you can hear how it sounds higher or lower. Repeat on all the different octaves to note the differences in sound.

The Black Keys

The black keys are different musical notes to the white keys. Play them, and you will notice a distinct difference. The names of these keys are also the same letters of the alphabet and take on the names of the white keys nearest them. The distinction is that keys to the left of the white key are known as flats and to the right of the white key are known as sharps. So, you have "B Sharp" or "B Flat," for example.

An easy way to remember this is to think about how your cutlery is laid out on the table. Your knife is sharp and always laid out to the right of your plate. That makes it easy to remember that right is sharp.

Now, because the black keys have a white key on either side of them, they can be called sharps or flats interchangeably. If you look to the right of a white "B" key on your keyboard, the black key is "C Sharp." But it is also left of the white "D" key and so is "D Flat." Don't overthink it too much – it is not all that important right now, and we go into it in more detail in Chapter 6 anyway.

What is more important is to learn your way around the keyboard – think more in terms of the letter, rather than it being a sharp or flat.

Quick Exercise: Now you know how to find your "C" and "F" notes and, because of this, how to find the others as well. Play each "C" note on the black and white keys and listen to how each sounds. Do the same for all the other keys as well.

Now try something a little more complicated. Position your thumb over any white key and your forefinger over the corresponding black key. Play each in quick succession. Then try playing them together. Experiment a little until you find the tones that match one another more closely.

Intervals

These are the distance between the different notes. A semitone, or half-step, will always separate the black key from the white key next to is. Where the white keys are not broken by black keys, like between "B" and "C" or "E" and "F", the difference in the note is a semitone.

A full tone is the space between two white keys that have a black key in between them, like "C" and "D".

Chapter Summary

- Your keyboard is made up of 52 white keys and 36 black keys. (Some older keyboards have fewer keys.)
- Each key represents a particular musical note.

- There are seven musical notes that we use in music – these are named A through to G.
- The black keys are grouped in twins or triplets to help you locate the different notes more easily.
- The white key to the left of a twin is always "C." The white key to the left of a triplet is always an "F."
- To remember the difference, remember that "C" has two points to it and "F" has three to it.
- The black keys take their names from the white keys closest to them.
- The black key to the right of a white key is called sharp. The one to the left of a white key is called flat.
- An easy way to remember this is that knives are sharp and are always put to the right of your plate when the table is laid.
- Intervals refer to the difference in sound between the white and black keys.

In the next chapter, you will learn about the pedals on your piano and how to use them.

Chapter Two: The Pedals

In this chapter, you will learn how and when to use the pedals on your piano. This is the second step in our seven-point plan in helping you learn to play the piano.

The pedals on the piano are not just there for decoration. You use the pedals for sounds that are not possible using just your hands. Most standard pianos will have two such foot pedals – the Una Corda on the left and the Sustain on the right. Some pianos have three pedals. The extra pedal in the middle is called the Sostenuto, but it is seldom used.

The Una Corda Pedal (The Soft Pedal)

Use your left foot to play this pedal. It helps to soften notes, so could be used when you are first starting to build up to a crescendo. It will not work on very loud notes, so the range is limited somewhat.

The Sustain Pedal

You will use your right foot with this pedal. It elongates your note's sound and causes it to resonate after you have lifted your fingers from the key. The resonance will be held until you take your foot off the pedal. This is usually used to bridge harmonies. With this pedal, as long as you are pressing the pedal, all the notes you play will be sustained.

The Sostenuto

As mentioned before, this is not something that you will use very often. You would normally use your right foot to play it, and it is similar to the Sustain Pedal in that it sustains the notes played. The difference between this pedal and the previous one is that the Sostenuto pedal only sustains the notes that you were playing when you pressed the pedals. Any notes played after that will play as normal.

Using the Pedals

When you start playing, get into position and position the balls of your feet above the pedals. Your heels should still touch the ground; this will help you maintain a good posture and also allow you to keep a light touch when it comes to depressing the pedals.

What you need to keep in mind is that this is not a stomping contest. You need to practice lifting your foot off the pedals gently. If you take your foot off too quickly, it can create a noisy bang; It can take a little practice to get used to using the pedals smoothly. Just think of it like parking your car – you don't smash the accelerator to the ground when parking, you ease into the parking slowly.

If the music calls for the use of the pedal, you will see the word "Ped" marked where you need to apply the pedal. Alternatively, the composition may call for the use of it all the way through the piece. You can release the pedal when you see an asterisk on the sheet. This will look like:

Quick exercise: Try using the pedals in conjunction with the lines of "It's Raining it's Pouring" that you learned in the previous chapter. Mix it up a little, play the same tune using the Una Corda pedal from time to time and then listen to how it sounds when you use the Sustain pedal instead. If you do have a Sostenuto panel, play around with that one as well.

Chapter Summary

- Most pianos have two pedals – the Una Corda pedal and the Sustain pedal.
- Some pianos have a third pedal – the Sostenuto pedal.
- The Una Corda pedal is always on the left; the Sustain pedal is always on the right. If the Sostenuto pedal is there, it will be in the middle.
- You will not use the Sostenuto pedal very often.
- The Una Corda pedal helps to soften notes.
- The Sustain pedal keeps the notes going for as long as you have the pedal down. It will do this for all notes played, while the pedal is down.
- The Sostenuto pedal isolates the note that was played when the pedal was first pressed and sustains only that particular note. The rest are played as normal.

In the next chapter, you will learn how to read some basic sheet music for yourself.

Chapter Three: Reading Sheet Music

In this chapter, you will learn what many of those dots and lines mean when it comes to sheet music. This is the third quick step in the program.

You need to know something about reading music in order to progress. Think of sheet music like a script for a movie, except that it is written using musical symbols rather than words. The composer could, technically, write out the words but it would make playing the music much slower and difficult because you would have to read each word.

Symbols are a lot easier to read, once you understand what they mean. The composer tells you which notes you should play, when to pause, how long to pause for, and even the pace at which you should play.

A sheet of music will look something like this:

Everything You Need to Know About a Piano Score

If you look at the score above, you will see a lot of dots, dashes, and other symbols. It looks a little confusing, but it's not so bad if you take it a note at a time. Each of the notes tells you which key you need to play and how long you need to play it for.

To keep the notes in some semblance of order, they are written on a five-line stave.

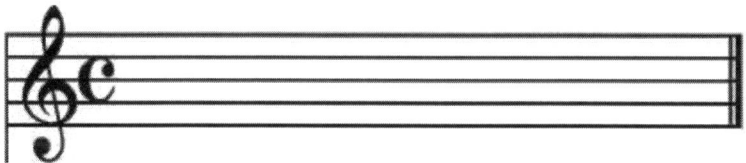

Starting with the Stave

The notes can be placed on the lines, or in the spaces between lines. Each line or space represents a specific note. The notes are divided up into equal sections called measured. These are separated from one another by bar lines – vertical lines at the end of that particular measure. The stave will normally start with some type of clef (The stylized "G" in the illustration above), and this may be followed by a sharp or a flat (The "C" in the illustration above.)

In addition, the markings above the stave will usually tell you what speed to play at. The markings underneath the stave will tell you what volume that section is to be played at.

You will see that there are usually two staves joined together with brackets, with different symbols at the top and bottom. This is known as a grand stave. It is denoted like this because you need to play both staves together – one set being the notes to play with your right hand, the other the notes to play with your left hand.

Don't worry about this too much at this stage – the main tune is usually shown in the stave for the right hand, so you don't need to pay attention to both now. In fact, as you will see later, you don't even have to have these two to play a tune so if you find it confusing, don't stress about it. We have a way around that.

The Basic Symbols to Learn

The Treble Clef

This is the stylized G that we were talking about in the previous section. There are a number of different ways that this is written. The treble clef shown below will denote which keys you need to play with your left hand. X

The treble clef looks like:

The Base Clef

This shows the part of the music to be played with your left hand. (To start out with, we are not going to worry too much about the left-hand section.) The base clef looks like:

The Key Signature

This is another thing that might appear at the start of the music. It shows which of the notes need to be played as flats and which need to be played as sharps.

This is what this will look like on your sheet music:

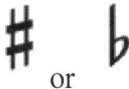
or

The Time Signature

This can be any two numbers. The numbers tell you how many beats there are in each measure. (We go over this in more detail in Chapter Seven.) This will look like:

$$\frac{2}{2}$$

Tempo Marking

This is a way of showing you what tempo the piece should be played at. The notation below shows the number of crotchet beats to play in a minute. Alternatively, they could write out what speed the piece is to be played at. This will often be in Italian like "Presto". (We go over each of these in more detail in Chapter 7).

This will look like:

=130

Dynamics

This lets you know what volume you need to play at. The "P" in the above diagram means Piano, or quiet. The "F" in the above means Forte or loudly. If the symbol has an "M" after it, it means moderate volume. (We are not really going to worry too much about that in these lessons though.) These symbols look like:

The Notes

These relate to the actual notes that you are playing so let's go into them in a little more detail. A note is generally

made up of a head (the dot) and a stem, the vertical line that is either above or below the dot. Your notes will look something like:

♩ ♩

Whole Notes

This is a whole note and will be one of the only ones that doesn't have a vertical line. This is meant to last four beats.

o

Half Notes

These are half notes or minimums and are played for two beats. You can tell that they are half notes because the dot is not filled in.

Quarter Notes

These are quarter notes – you will normally play four of these in one measure. (More about that in Chapter Seven).

Quavers and Semi-Quavers

These are eighth notes or quavers and sixteen notes or semiquavers.

Where the Notes Are Displayed

There are two shortcuts that you can use to remember which line or space each note is displayed in. Remember how we said that some of the notes are displayed on the lines, and some are displayed in the spaces in between them, this is how you remember what notes go where.

For The Lines

Remember the mnemonic device, Every Good Boy Deserves Fruit. In this case, the "E" note is recorded on the top line, the "G" note on the next line down, the "B" note on the middle line, the "D" note on the next line down and the "F" note on the final line.

For The Spaces

Remember the word FACE to keep this one straight but this time start from the space at the bottom and work your way up. So, the "F" note is in the final space of the stave, the "A" note is in the next space up, the "C" note is in the space second from the top, and the "E" note is in the space right at the top of the stave. In this case, the "F" note is an octave lower than in the previous example.

A Quick Shortcut

I am now going to teach you a shortcut to playing popular music. This only works with music that has words to it, but it is a great shortcut and is more than enough if you just want to be able to play some tunes for the family.

The sheet music example we displayed previously was made up of grand staves. When you have lyrics as well, these are displayed in the vocal line. This is a stave that is directly above the grand staves and is a much more simplified version of the notes. It will usually have a treble stave at the very front.

If you want to start playing music quickly and easily, concentrate on the vocal line only. This allows you to play at the pace that suits you and is a lot easier than having to read the more complex staves beneath it.

The additional advantage of doing this is that you can buy music sheets that only have the vocal line on them. If your main aim is to be able to play a few tunes, this can save you a lot of money and space because the grand staves are not usually included in these copies.

Quick Exercise: Go to http://www.music-for-music-teachers.com/silent-night-sheet-music.html, and you can download the sheet music for "Silent Night" for free, in a simple format. It's a fairly simple composition and one that you probably already know the melody for. See how well you can follow along on your piano.

Chapter Summary

- You need to know what the different symbols on sheet music are in order to be able to interpret it.
- Sheet music is set out in a five-line stave. You can see which note to play based on where it is placed in the stave and also the symbol used.
- Things like the general tempo of the piece will be listed at the beginning of the stave.
- Notations above and below the stave can show the speed at which a piece is to be played and what volume to play it at.
- A stave will usually consist of at least two separate sections, one for the notes to be played with the left hand and one for the notes to be played with the right hand. These two staves should be played at the same time and so are bracketed together to form a grand stave. (We are not going to do that right now, though.)
- The symbol for the note will tell you what note to play and how long to play it for.
- Each note is displayed on a different line, or space, in the stave.
- An easy way to remember which note goes on which line is to remember "Every Boy Deserves Good Fruit." This is read from the top line to the bottom one.

- An easy way to remember which note goes into what space, is to remember the word "FACE." In this case, the spaces are read from the bottom up. The notes used in this case are an octave lower than in the previous instance.
- To make things a lot easier for yourself, you can read the music from the vocal line. This is a much more simplified stave meant to be read by singers so it does not have all the symbols a grand stave would have and does not have them separated into notes to be played by the left hand and notes to be played by the right hand.

In the next chapter, you will learn about more about practicing scales and why it is not a boring time waster.

Chapter Four: Practising Scales

In this chapter, you will learn about scales and why you should look forward to practicing them. This is your fourth lesson – you are almost there now.

Now that you understand about which keys are which, know when to use the pedals and know something about reading sheet music, we are ready to move on to playing scales. This is the fourth step in our program.

How did you do with playing "Silent Night?" It should have been relatively simple for you – you might have made a mistake or two here or there, but, overall, you should have been able to follow it. See how easy it is to start playing real music? And you can play popular songs like that without ever having to worry about learning scales.

However, there is a good reason that one of the first things you normally learn to play on a piano are scales. Now, admittedly, this can seem a little boring, but it is good practice. Scales are a great way for you to build up a working knowledge of the melodies in a song and to also give your fingers more practice. So, while you can play without practicing scales, if you really want to start getting better, you will have to spend some time on this.

The most important thing about scales is that you should repeat them over and over again. Think of it like a putting green in golf – you are there to practice your swing, not to actually play a game. The more you practice, however, the better your swing gets and the better you are able to play when you actually head out to the course. The same applies for practicing scales on your piano.

What is a Scale?

It is a series of notes that follow on from one another in a particular order. The most commonly encountered scales are major scales and minor scales. They both have the following commonalities:

- They are both eight notes in length.
- The topmost note and the bottommost note are only an octave apart.
- Each note is done in order from lowest to highest or highest to lowest. You do not mix up the order of the notes at all.
- Scales are made up of a combination of half- or whole steps.

If you understand how the scales work, you are able to build any type of scale you want, just by adding in the right sequence of steps. Scales form the basis for creating chords and allowing you to learn to improvise. You will need to know these if you want to start composing your own music.

The scales that you choose to practice will be dependent on what musical style you are most interested in.

It is, however, a good idea to start by learning the major scales and then move on to practicing the minor scales.

Major Scales

The pattern here will be a tone, a tone, a semitone, a tone, atone, a tone, and a semitone. It is pretty easy to work out, as long as you start on the right note. All major scales will be based on the same principle.

You can, for example, play an "C" scale in major. You can start on "C" and then move up through the other notes, using only the white keys. The "C" major scale is one of the easiest to start with because you only need to concentrate on the white keys.

Major scales are generally thought to be livelier in nature.

Minor Scales

Once you are more comfortable with major scales, you can try your hand at minor scales. The minor scales are available in three separate versions – the harmonic or the natural or the melodic scales. What this means is that every minor scale has three separate formats to learn.

The Natural Minor Scales

This is the key minor scale to practice. The difference between it and your major scale is that you start with the A note and then finish off again with the A note.

The Harmonic Minor Scales

This also follows a set pattern, but it is slightly different. It is a tone, a semitone, a tone, a tone, a semitone, a tone + a half and a semitone. This pattern is often described as a bit eerie in nature and will lend something of a haunting quality to your work.

The Melodic Minor Scales

This is more complex because you will use the pattern, a tone, a tone, a semitone, atone, a tone, a semitone and then a tone when working your way up the scales. When working your way back, it changes to a tone, a tone, a semitone, a tone, a tone, a semitone, and finishes on tone.

What makes this scale useful, is that it teaches you to be more flexible when it comes to your other scales. When practicing your minor scales, it is best to start with the A minor scales because these are easiest.

Quick Exercise: Practice this now - find the Middle C and practice working your way through all seven notes. You would start by using your thumb and the rest of the fingers on your right hand and then bring in your left hand for the final two keys. Practice this working your way up the scales, and then down them again.

When you have mastered that, you can move on to practicing more scales. You can try starting with a different note, always remembering to move up either half a step or a whole step. Here is an illustration of the different C Scales that you can use to get you started with your practicing.

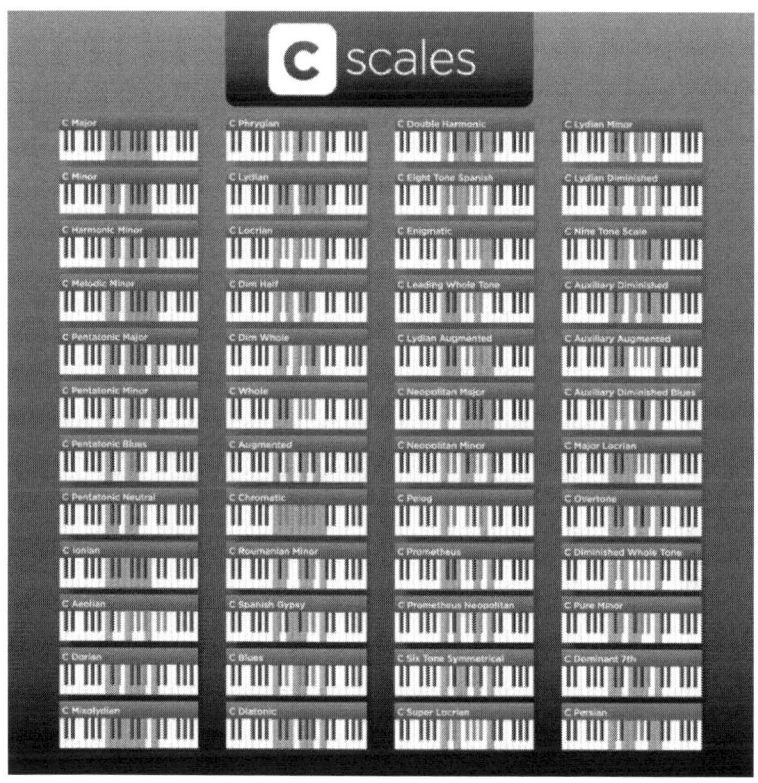

Most of the C scales shown above can be accomplished using your right hand only. It is also important to practice scales using your left hand, so don't just focus on one type. Try to practice at least three different scales a day for at least ten minutes overall in order to get better at them.

Chapter Summary

- Scales are seen by a lot of people as boring, but they are essential exercises when it comes to getting to know the keys.
- They can also be used as warmups or to help build up the strength in your finger.
- The key to getting scales right is to know your intervals really well. Every successive key is either a half- or whole step up or down from the previous one.
- There are minor scales and major scales, each with their own unique pattern.
- There are three varieties of minor scales – the natural, harmonic and melodic.

In the next chapter, you will learn about using chords to make the melodies sound richer.

Chapter Five: Adding in Chords

In this chapter, you will learn about adding in chords. This is the fifth step in the program.

Chords are important in creating harmonies. You will distinguish them on your music sheet because they will have three or four notes stacked on top of one another.

What is a Chord?

A chord is made up of at least three tones, played simultaneously, where the intervals are based on a set formula. So, slamming your fingers down on four or five random keys may be fun, but is not a chord.

Three-Note Chords

These are the simplest ones to work with and are also known as triads. You will normally play these by using your pinky, thumb, and forefinger. Chords begin very simply. Like melodies, chords are based on scales.

Chords are essentially based on scales, the difference being that with scales, each note is played in succession. With chords, all of the notes are played together.

The root note is the note that you start with. The chord will be named for this note. If you are using a basic triad, you will have your root note and two other notes, notes that are at a third interval from the first note and at the fifth interval from the first note.

You can add to the chord by moving up a step or a half-step, or by adding extra notes in. To make things easier for you, though, I have included a list of all the basic chords at the end of this chapter.

Major Chords

These are the ones that you will use most often and are the easiest to play. A lot of the songs that you play, including Silent Night, consist of major chords. Major chords are based on your major scales. The first example in the illustration below is an example of a major chord.

Most of the time, composers will omit writing "Major" when using a chord. They simply use the symbol for chord above the staff of it to show which chord it is. If you see the symbol for a chord, and nothing naming it, you can assume that it is a major chord.

Other Chords You May Encounter

You are mostly going to be dealing with major or minor chords, but that does not mean that these are all that there is. Other chords are formed by adding extra notes to your standard major or minor chord.

Augmented Chords And Diminished Chords

The only real difference in a major or minor chord is the third interval. The fifth interval, however, is always the same and it is here that you can play around to create a new chord altogether.

Augmented chords consist of the root note, your major third interval, and an augmented fifth interval. With augmented chords, you raise the final note by another half-step and always work with a major chord to start with. Here are examples of augmented chords.

Piano Chords — Augmented

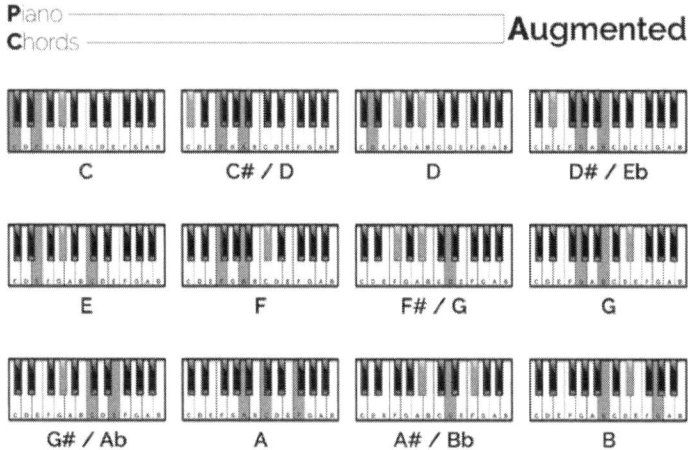

Diminished chords consist of the root note, your minor third interval, and your diminished fifth interval. In this case, you lower the final note by half a step and always work with a minor chord to start with. You would normally see them with "Dim" in the name.

Here are some examples of diminished chords:

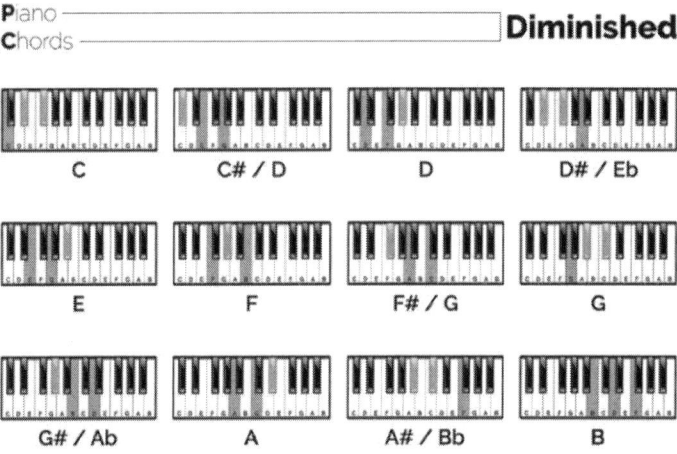

Suspended Chords

This is considered a three-note chord, but it is not really a triad. In this case, one of the notes is left hanging, meaning that you need to wait for the next one. There are two options when it comes to suspended chords – The second and fourth suspended chords. They will have "Sus" in the name.

A suspended two chord is made up of the root note, the major second interval, and the fifth interval. A suspended four chord is made up of the root note, the fourth interval, and the fifth interval.

Generally speaking, a suspended chord will usually be followed by another note, but they can also be used on their own.

Here are examples of suspended chords:

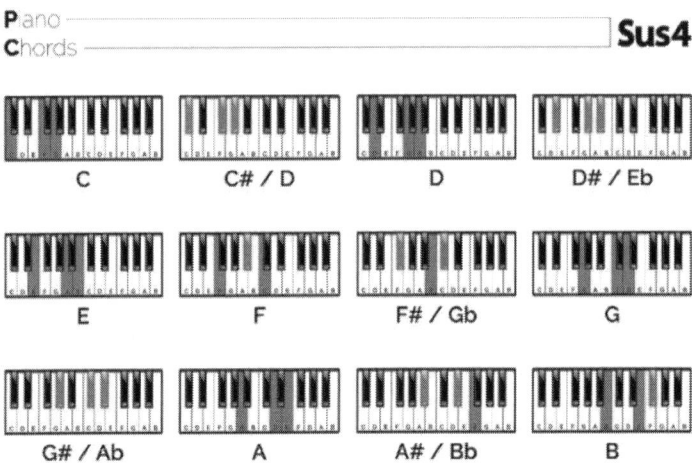

Adding a Seventh Interval

A triad is a basic kind of chord. In order to make it more interesting, you can add other notes at the end in the form of a seventh interval. It is usually used in a composition to help create suspense and will usually be followed by a major chord or minor chord. On its own, it is not likely to sound great, but when added to a triad, it improves the sound.

You can choose to add any of the chords we have discussed here to create this seventh interval.

The Chord Symbols

Chord symbols let you know the type of chord and what the root note of the chord is. These will start with the letter of the root note. (Keep in mind that with a major chord, this will be all there is.)

With other chords, you will have either a letter in the name, such as "M" to indicate a minor chord and/ or a letter like "7" to indicate the seventh chord. So, if, for example, you see the name Dm6, you know you have that you are playing the D minor chord with a sixth interval.

The chord is played along with the note that is shown underneath it. You will hold this chord until you see a new chord symbol or change of cord marked in the music.

Chord Inversions

It's not the most interesting exercise to play the same chords over and over again. You really don't need to do this at all. It doesn't matter what you do with the basic chords; they will always sound exactly the same.

That is where chord inversions come into play. They allow you to change up the sound of a chord. So instead of playing the root chord, and following it with the third chord and fifth chord, as usual, you could change things up by starting with the final chord and ending on the root chord.

So now what you are doing is to play the root chord an octave higher than the standard chords.

Inversions can also help you to transition from one chord to the next. Let's say you are playing a C major chord, followed by an A minor chord. This would mean playing the C chord and then moving your hand over to play the next set of keys – it would be somewhat clumsy.

If you use an inversion, though, your hand will end up in the correct position as you end off the C chord, allowing you to play with a lot less effort.

Using Chord Progressions

Chord progression means moving through a range of chords in the same key signature. Imagine how boring it would be if you played the same chord throughout the entire piece. You can use chord progressions to liven things up a bit or to move from one signature to the next.

Arpeggios

You don't always have to play the notes that make up your chord at the same time. You can also rather play them one after another in sequence. Arpeggios help to keep the piece moving. You would, for example, instead of playing a typical C major chord, play each note, starting with the

"C," individually. You would then play the "C" in the next octave before reversing the order of play and going back down to the first "C" you played.

This would just be one possible version so try changing it up a bit. This is also possible using minor chords – you just would not need to descend at the end of the structure again.

A Round-Up of Different Chords That You Might Come Across

Chapter Summary

- Chords are notes that are played together to create a more harmonious composition.
- On the music sheet, a chord is denoted if there are three notes stacked together.
- Chords are at least three notes long and are calculated according to set formulae rather than just being chosen at random.
- A chord is usually based on the scales that you use.
- There are many different kinds of chords.
- Augmented chords are created from major scales and have the last note going up by half a step.
- Diminished chords are created from minor scales and have the last note dropping by half a step. They will have "Dim" in their name.
- Suspended chords leave you hanging and need to be finished off with another note. They will have "Sus" in their name.
- You can add another interval in order to make the chord more interesting.
- Major chords are named after their root note. So, a C major cord is simply named "C."
- You can invert cords to make them more interesting and to make the play smoother. This means starting with your top note and

carrying on into the next octave with your root note.
- Chord progressions can make the piece more interesting and can help bridge one signature line with another.
- Arpeggios are another way to change things up – you play exactly the same notes, except this time you change things up by playing the notes in sequence rather than together.

In the next chapter, you will learn more about sharps and flats.

Chapter Six: Sharps and Flats

In this chapter, you will learn how to start incorporating the black keys and how to recognize when to do so. This is your sixth lesson.

The symbols that we deal with in this chapter are also known as accidentals. These "accidentals" tell you when to use the black keys, or how to modify your note's pitch.

As mentioned previously, the black keys are called sharps or flats, and named for the white keys directly next to them. Let's do a quick recap. If the black key is to the right of the white key, it will be that key's sharp. If it is to the left of that key, it will be that key's flat.

Here's a diagram of how this would look on your actual keyboard:

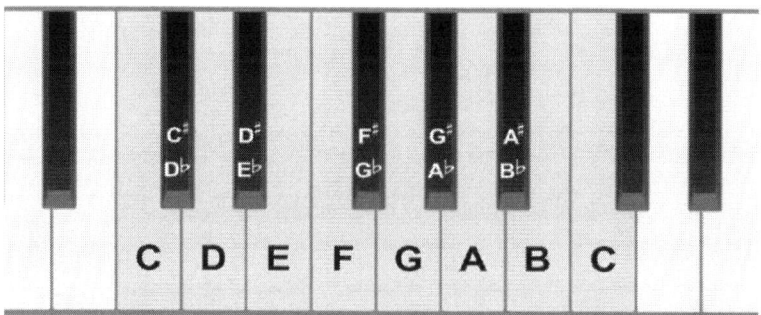

On the sheet music, you will see the symbol for the sharp or the flat directly before the note, next to the head of the note that it applies to.

Sharps

Sharps raise the pitch by a half-step or semitone. The symbol for a sharp is:

Flats

Flats lower the pitch by a half-step or semitone. The symbol for a flat is:

♭

The Natural Key

This tells you that it is time to stop using the black keys. It will precede the natural note and tell you that you should play all the remaining notes in that series as natural notes. The symbol for the natural key is:

♮

The Key Signature

You will also see these notes directly after the clef or base staves and before any time signature. This is what is referred to as the key signature, and it lets you know what key to use for the tune, and how many sharps and flats there are in the piece. You will need to look this over before starting.

Once you have been practicing your scales, this gets a whole lot simpler to do. All of the keys except for A minor and C major have both flats and sharps.

Chapter Summary

- Accidentals are used to change the pitch of notes – they change the pitch by a half-tone or semitone.
- The three accidentals are Flat, Sharp and Natural.
- To get the flat and sharp notes, you have to use the black keys on the keyboard.
- The flat takes its name from the white key to its left and reduces the pitch.
- The sharp takes its name from the black key to its right and increases the pitch.
- So, every black key is both a sharp and a flat.
- The natural symbol tells you to revert to stop using the black keys.

In the next chapter, you will learn why timing is so important and how you can get this critical aspect right.

Chapter Seven: It's All About the Timing

In this chapter, you will learn the final and possibly most important element in this book – how to get the timing right. This is the final step in our program.

There is more to music than getting the notes and chords right. (Sure, that is obviously a big piece of the puzzle, but you also need to be able to get the timing and beat right.) In fact, you might be able to slip an incorrect chord or note past your audience without them noticing, but they will notice immediately if your timing is off.

The timing of the notes is what makes the music happy or sad. If we never adjusted the tempo at which we played, every piece of music would sound pretty much the same. Each note has a point where it starts and a point where it ends. As a result, we need to assign values to this length that we are able to count. In this chapter, we are going to learn how to really get the rhythm going and keep it going.

The Beat

When you are listening to music and clapping along or tapping your foot in time with it, the beat is what you are trying to keep up with. The faster the beat, the faster and more energetic the song. The slower the beat, the slower the music is. Getting the tempo, or how fast the beat is, right is extremely important.

Use Tempo to Measure the Beat

When it comes to music, time gets measured in beats. In this case, the number of beats per minute. If you want a piece to sound correct, you need to pay attention to the beat.

Quick Exercise: Get out your smartphone and set the timer for a minute. Every two seconds, tap your foot once. That's a beat. Now, you can speed this up by increasing the number of taps to one per second, or slow it down to one tap every three seconds. That's the tempo.

In the exercise above, the first beat was 30 beats per minute because you tapped your foot 30 times. The second beat was 20 beats per minute because you slowed it down. In both cases, the beat was steady because you were timing your taps to the second.

When reading music, you would refer to the tempo marking to tell you what speed to play the music at. This will either be in the form of either a written word to tell you what pace to use, or a metronome marking that will tell you exactly how many beats per minute.

You can follow the guidelines in the table below to see what the basic readings are in terms of tempo.

Written	Translation	Number of Beats Per Minute
Largo	Very Slow	40 – 60
Adagio	Slow	61 - 72
Andante	Moderate	73 – 96
Allegro	Fast	97 - 132
Vivace	Faster	133 – 168
Presto	Very Fast	169 - 208

Measuring Tempo

When you are playing a piece of music, you won't be able to check your smartphone to see how many seconds have elapsed. A metronome is a handy device that can help you instead. You set it to the rate that you like, and it will tick out the rhythm accordingly.

The Grouping of Beats

Remember how I said earlier that the sheet of music was like a script? Every note is recorded in the order that it is meant to be played in. Unlike a script, however, the stave can be divided up into equal sections of time. These smaller sections make it possible to check the beat and to understand whereabouts you are in the actual composition.

Now, in a slower tempo song, this might not be much of a problem, but when it comes to faster-paced music, you could have a few hundred different beats in just a few minutes. Keeping track of the beat in this manner would mean counting high numbers when you are trying to concentrate on what you are doing.

It would become difficult to do this, so composers have come up with a workaround. Instead, the music is divided up into measures – smaller bits that are easier to keep track of. The number of beats in a measure will normally be decided by the composer, and this can change. They will indicate the end of a measure by drawing a vertical line, or bar line, through all the lines and spaces of the stave. This will look something like:

Most compositions, however, will have four beats per measure. This means that you would just have to count to four each time when playing – not too difficult a task. The measures break the music into segments or patterns that we can then use to help determine the time signature of the piece.

The Rhythm of Melody

Without the melody of notes played, the beat wouldn't mean much at all. The different lengths of the notes are what makes the music more interesting. It's like listening to a good public speaker – they change the cadence of their voice and mix up the tones so that it sounds more interesting.

In contrast, if the speaker just spoke in a monotone, without varying the tone or rhythm, it wouldn't be long before everyone became bored with the speech. The same is true of music.

Some music is very distinctive – you can recognize the tune just by hearing the beat. Take "Jingle Bells" for example – you don't have to hear it being played on an instrument to recognize it, you could tap out the beat with your foot, and someone would still recognize it.

We said earlier that you could get away with not having to read all the characters on a standard music sheet. You do, however, need to know exactly how much time every note is meant to last for. At the beginning of the piece, the composer lets you know how many equal pieces to divide each measure into. That means working out fractions but, in this case, it's not hard.

Think of it like cutting up a pizza. You can divide the pizza up into halves, quarters or eighths, or more if you like. When it comes to music, this usually translates into four pieces of "pizza" per measure. Or, more accurately, four quarter notes, or four beats. This is represented by the most common music symbol:

♩♩

You will always know if a note is a quarter note because the head will always be completely black. In our example, you have divided the pizza up into four equal slices and are eating just one, so it is finished faster. In the same way, the notes are played faster and not held for as long.

Quick Exercise: Set your metronome to one beat per second. Every time it clicks, play one-quarter note in whichever key you prefer. Stick to a single note, for now, say for example, "C" so that you can get the hang of playing to the beat. Every time the metronome clicks, hit the "C" key. Get this right before moving on to the next section.

Half Notes

Alternatively, you could choose to divide the pizza into halves and eat one piece again. You will take longer to eat the pizza because there is more of it. By a similar token, half notes are longer than quarter notes, so you would divide the measure up into two instead of four. So, it would now be two beats per measure instead of just one.

This would be represented on the sheet as follows:

𝅗𝅥 𝅘𝅥

Quick Exercise: Set your metronome to one beat per second again, and this time, play a note on every second click. You would hold the key down for the count of these two beats.

Why do the Stems Get Displayed Differently?

You will notice in the examples above, that there are two ways to show the stem of a note – either pointing up or pointing down. Why is that? Any notes that are either on the middle line of the stave or above it, will have their stems underneath the note head and to the right. Any notes that fall below this will have the stems above the note head and to the left.

This helps to make a clearer distinction between the notes on different lines. If all the notes were just circles, it would be a lot harder to keep your place when reading the music quickly.

Whole Notes

A whole note lasts the entire measure for a count of four. So, back to our pizza example, if you ate the whole thing, it would take longer.

It is a simple circle and looks like this:

o

Playing a whole note is pretty simple, just count to four and then play the note. You would just need to make sure that the note lasts for the length of the measure.

Quick Exercise: Set your metronome to one beat per second and again, hold down any key you like. Hold it down for the count of four clicks and then move on to play the next note.

Putting It All Together

Now that you know how the count works, and know how long to hold the keys down for and what the basic note values are, you can start playing around a little and we can move onto the more complex notes.

Again, if you were only to stick to full, half and quarter notes, there would only be so much variation that you would be able to achieve. You can divide it up even more to fit in more notes per measure and increase the tempo.

You don't actually change the speed, but you are holding the notes down for smaller periods at a time. It may take some getting used to so, if you are battling, to keep up, slow things down a bit by slowing the speed of your playing. As you get more used to this rate, and more familiar with the eighth notes, and sixteenth notes, you can start to speed up again.

Eighth Notes

Eighth notes are also known as quavers. This is like your pizza into eight pieces. To eat a piece won't take as long as it would if you were eating half the pizza because you are getting much less pizza. By the same token, you just need to hold the note down for a lot less time, and move faster through the notes in the same measure. Instead of fitting 4-beats into a measure, you need to fit in eight so you will need to speed up your metronome. The symbol for an eighth note is:

If there are two or more of these notes, the flag changes to a solid beam and connects the notes. This helps in making the beat a lot more obvious. It will look something like this:

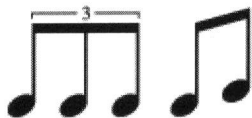

Sixteenth Notes

Sixteenth notes are also known as semi-quavers. The same rule applies to sixteenth notes. Like with eighth notes, when they are by single notes, they are shown with flags – except this time there are two flags.

When there are more than one of these in a row, the flags are changed to beams, as follows:

It is quite common to see four such notes placed together in this way because that represents one beat. You might also find it joined with an eighth note as follows:

Now, if you can slow things down a lot, it is pretty easy to play these notes. However, if you play them at the tempo that they are meant to be played at, it starts getting more complicated. That said, with practice, you will be fine to play these notes as well.

And dividing up the beat doesn't stop at sixteenths, some composers go a step further and halve it again so that it is 32nds, 64ths or 128ths. They show this in the composition by increasing the number of flags. I am not going to go into examples here because these are not as common as the eighth notes and sixteenth notes and should be left until you have had a bit more practice.

Rests

No matter how much practice you have, there is only a certain amount that you will be able to do. Your fingers are going to need a break from time to time and so will your audience. These breaks can be quick or a little longer, but the defining character of them is that you are not playing anything. You continue to count the beat, but you don't actually play or hold any kind of note.

In orchestral compositions, this will often be where the strings take over or someone playing another instrument gets their own solo. All you need to do is to relax your hands and keep them poised over the keys and make sure that you keep up with the count. Just like there are different note lengths, there are different rest periods. Let's have a look at these.

Whole And Half Rests

Let's say that you are playing a whole "C". You press the key and keep it depressed for a count of four beats. When you are playing half note, you keep it down for half as long. Rests will work in a similar fashion – you won't play anymore for the same number of beats.

I like to think of the symbol for the whole rest as a comfortable bed that you can sink into. You would relax for a decent period. It will always be on the fourth line or above so that it is easier to spot. It looks like this:

▃

The half rest is the same symbol, turned upside down. So, still a bed but a little less comfortable. It will always sit on the middle line. It looks like this:

▃

Quarter Rests and Beyond

These are the same as your quarter, eighth and sixteenth notes in terms of timing. Here are the symbols – from left to right, these are the symbols for the quarter, eighth and sixteenth rest respectively.

𝄽 𝄾 𝄿

Time Signatures

In music, a time signature is what you use to find out the meter of the piece. The time signature is split into two numbers; the top number number tells you the meter of the piece you're playing. So, if the number is 4 over 4, that means there are four quarter note beats. If it is 2 over 2, there are two half note beats.

If the composer wants to use more than one type of note, like one-half note and two-quarter notes, that is fine – they could show this as 2 over 4 and 1 over 2. They do need to ensure that the top number adds up to a whole number in the end. So, one-half note and two-quarter notes, if we add them mathematically, would total 4 quarters in total and this makes sense.

If the composer tried to say three-quarter notes and one-half note, you would end up with too many beats, and this would not work. So, you should never see a time signature that is something like 5 over 4.

Common Time

Most composers stick to common time, i.e., 4 over 4. They indicate this by using the letter "C" in place of the standard time signature. It will appear directly after the clef symbol of the stave. This is how this would be displayed within the stave:

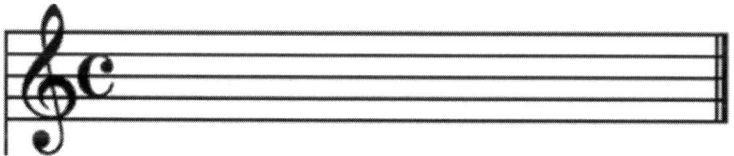

Chapter Summary

- The beat needs to be measured and kept at a steady pace.
- The faster the tempo that the notes are played at, the more energetic the pace of the piece.
- Beats are grouped in measures. These break up the music into equal sections. The

composer will decide how many beats to use per measure.
- A whole note will take up a full measure, or four full beats. So, you would hold the note for the full length of that measure and only press the note once during that particular measure.
- A half note is half as long so there will be two beats in one measure.
- The notes can be divided into quarters, eighths and sixteenths as well. Each of these is shorter than the last so there will be more notes to play within each measure. This means that as the tempo increases the smaller the notes get.
- If you are still learning, slow down the tempo until you get used to playing the notes in the right succession. Then you can start worrying about speeding up again.
- The stems of the notes are arbitrary, used more as a way of differentiating the notes than having a very specific meaning.
- Rests are just as important when it comes to playing – they give you time to have a break and also give your audience a little break as well.
- A rest is usually similar in length to the note preceding it. The main thing to remember is to keep track of the beat.
- During a rest, keep your hands relaxed but poised at the ready for the next lot of notes.

Final Words

Well done – you have completed the program. Learning to play the piano can be fun, and it really is not that hard once you know the basics. It's a simple seven-step process:

- Step One: Learn the Keyboard and the keys.
- Step Two: Learn how and when to use the pedals.
- Step Three: Learn something about reading sheet music.
- Step Four: Practice your scales.
- Step Five: Learn about adding chords.
- Step Six: Learn when to use sharps and flats.
- Step Seven: Learn to get the tempo right.

In this book, we have started you off on the basics you need to play your first full composition. You should now be able to play some simple tunes and impress your friends with how fast your learned this skill.

From now forward, all it takes to really master the piano is to practice, and you get to decide how far you want to go. You can choose to practice every day, or trot your skills out on high days and holidays – it really is completely up to you.

Image Credit: Shutterstock.com

More by Preston Hoffman

Discover all books from the Music Best Seller Series by Preston Hoffman at:

bit.ly/preston-hoffman

Book 1: *Music Theory*

Book 2: *How to Read Music*

Book 3: *How to Play Guitar*

Book 4: *How to Play Ukulele*

Book 5: *How to Play Piano*

Book 6: *How to Play Chords*

Book 7: *How to Play Scales*

Themed book bundles available at discounted prices:

bit.ly/preston-hoffman

Printed in Great
Britain
by Amazon